FISCAL YEAR 2013

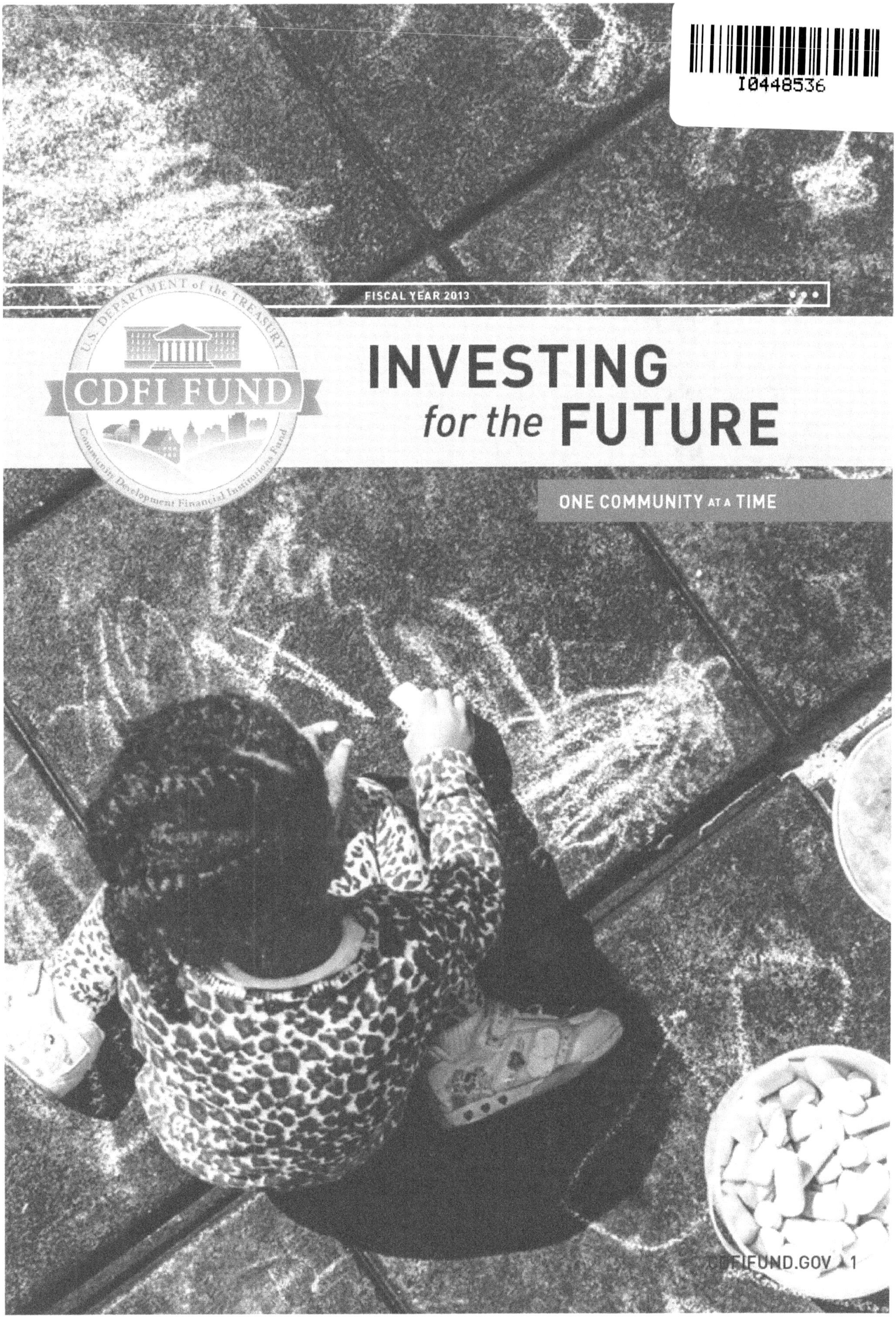

INVESTING
for the FUTURE

ONE COMMUNITY AT A TIME

CDFIFUND.GOV 1

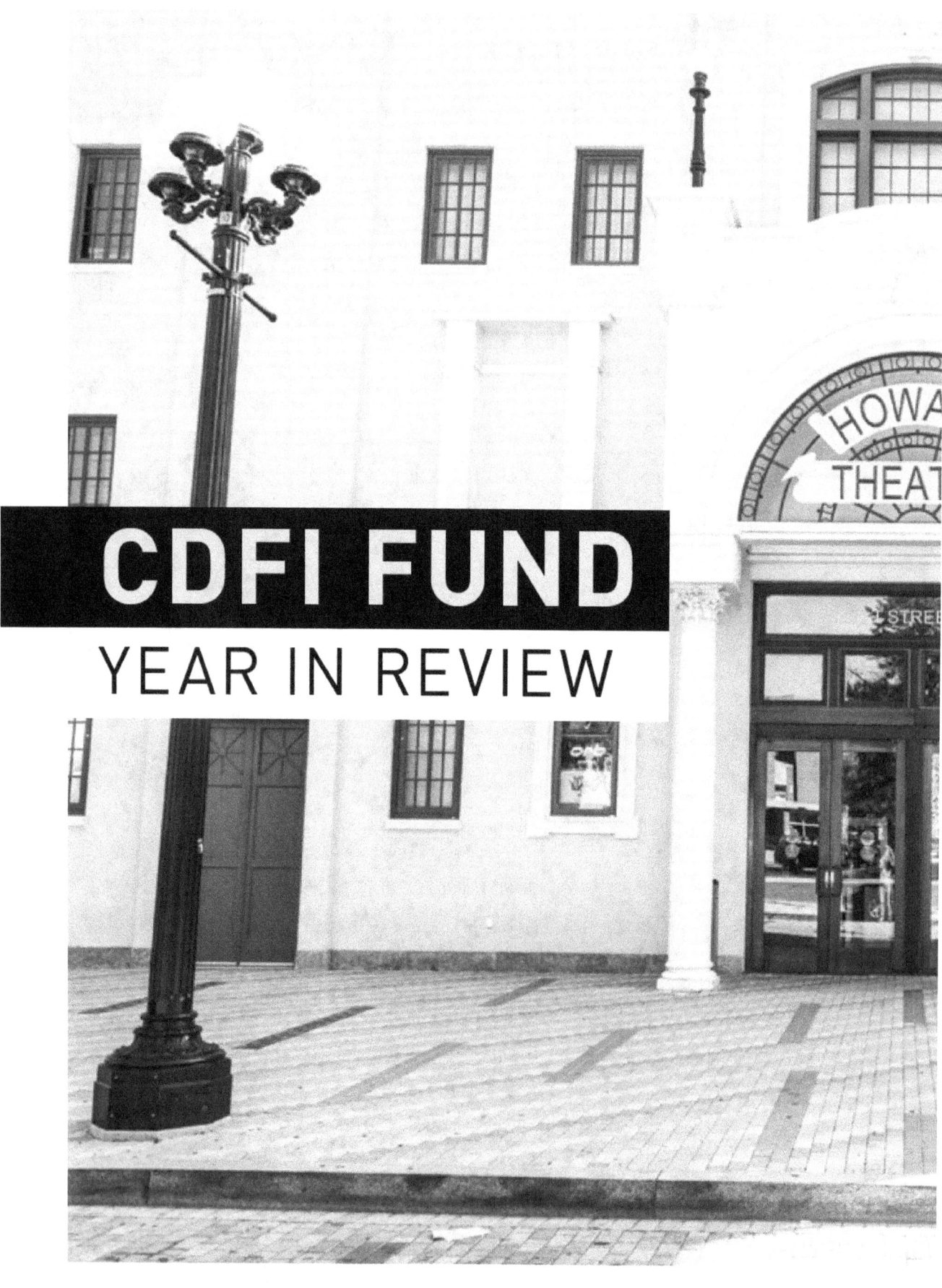

CDFI FUND
YEAR IN REVIEW

TABLE OF CONTENTS

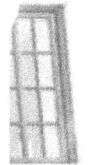

INTRODUCTION
& OVERVIEW

SOUND ADVICE: INVESTING FOR THE FUTURE

A REFLECTION ON FY 2013

A financial planner will tell you that investing for the future is critical. This involves not only taking a realistic assessment of where you are presently, but envisioning the future and building a plan to support that vision. So it is with an eye toward the future that in fiscal year (FY) 2013 the Community Development Financial Institutions Fund (CDFI Fund) focused on analyzing its impact, enhancing its processes, incorporating new programs, and strengthening the integrity of what it means to be a Community Development Financial Institution (CDFI).

At a time when research reports continue to demonstrate the slower pace of economic recovery in low-income and minority communities, CDFIs and Community Development Entities (CDEs) are more important than ever to revitalizing economically underserved communities across the country.

The CDFI Fund's "2013 Year in Review" showcases the impact of the CDFI Fund's programs. Supporting CDFIs is integral to realizing the CDFI Fund's vision of economically empowering America's underserved and distressed communities.

The CDFI Fund awarded $185 million to 236 organizations for the FY 2013 rounds of the cornerstone Community Development Financial Institutions Program (CDFI Program) and the Native American CDFI Assistance Program (NACA Program), including $22 million through the Healthy Food Financing Initiative. The CDFI Fund also awarded $3.5 billion in allocation authority to Community Development Entities (CDEs) under the calendar year (CY) 2012 round of the New Markets Tax Credit Program (NMTC Program) and selected 85 FDIC-insured institutions to receive approximately $17 million in the FY 2013 round of the Bank Enterprise Award Program (BEA Program).

Growing a nationwide network of institutions focused on community development finance in low-incomes areas was the central purpose of the legislation that created the CDFI Fund almost 20 years ago. And ever since then, certification as a CDFI is the first step an organization will take in order to participate in the CDFI Fund's programs. Certification confirms that a financial institution has a track record in principally serving a clearly identified low-income community by providing both financing and development services, and that it is accountable to that community. Many private sector and governmental partners value this certification.

VISION AND MISSION

The CDFI Fund's vision is to economically empower America's underserved and distressed communities.

Its mission is to increase economic opportunity and promote community development investments for underserved populations and in distressed communities in the United States.

Recognizing how important certification is, in 2013 the CDFI Fund undertook to recertify all existing CDFIs if their most recent certification was more than three years old. This formal recertification process was both an investment in the integrity of the certification status for organizations and a way to position the CDFI Fund's certification policies for the future. During FY 2013, the CDFI Fund recertified 425 CDFIs and certified 76 new CDFIs. Including CDFIs that were not required to recertify in 2013, the CDFI Fund ended the fiscal year with a total of 811 certified CDFIs, including 67 Native CDFIs.

In FY 2013 the CDFI Fund launched the CDFI Bond Guarantee Program, which opened in June. The CDFI Bond Guarantee Program has the potential to transform the CDFI industry by injecting substantial new long-term capital into our nation's most distressed communities. In September, the CDFI Fund announced the approval of the term sheets and the execution of agreements to guarantee $325 million in bonds. Bond proceeds will enable Eligible CDFIs to make loans in low-income and distressed communities across the country.

2013 also saw the beginning of a rigorous, evidence-based evaluation of the impact of the CDFI Program. Specifically, the study, which will be released later this year, will look at the financial performance and social impacts of the CDFI Program. This will be the first time the CDFI Fund has undertaken such research. In addition, the CDFI Fund commenced an analysis of the "Access to Capital and Credit in Native Communities," a follow up to a 2001 report on Native American, Alaskan Native, and Native Hawaiian communities that established some of the key guidelines of the CDFI Fund's Native Initiatives.

The results of this research will allow the CDFI Fund to better assess its programs and how it can better serve communities in the years ahead.

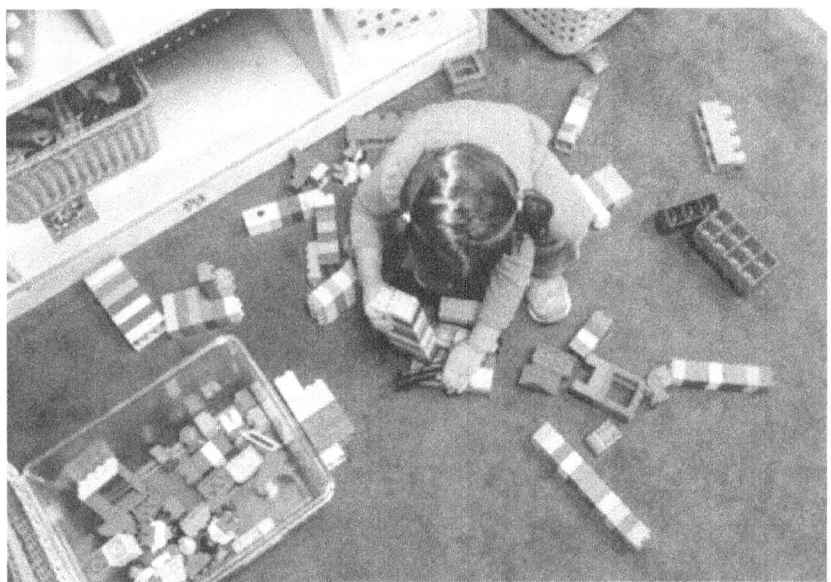

In addition, the CDFI Fund continued its efforts to strengthen the oversight of award recipients by: hiring additional staff for the Office of Certification, Compliance Monitoring and Evaluation (CCME); developing a framework for a risk-based approach to compliance management; and reinstituting compliance site visits and desk audits of awardees.

Investing today puts you in a better position to meet your long-term goals. The work of the CDFI Fund highlighted throughout this Year In Review represents not only the hard work and passion of CDFI Fund's staff, but also its long-term commitment to America's underserved and distressed communities as sources of economic opportunity and growth for their residents and the nation.

CDFI FUND OVERVIEW

The CDFI Fund, part of the U.S. Department of the Treasury, plays a unique and important role in generating economic growth in America.

By fostering the creation and expanding the capacity of CDFIs and by supporting the work of other community development organizations and insured depository institutions, the CDFI Fund helps build businesses, create jobs, and revitalize communities.

The CDFI Fund achieves its purpose by promoting access to capital and local economic growth through the following programs:

- Community Development Financial Institutions Program
- Native Initiatives
- New Markets Tax Credit Program
- CDFI Bond Guarantee Program
- Bank Enterprise Award Program

The CDFI Fund is the only Federal government entity whose primary focus is to build the capacity of CDFIs so that they can provide loans, investments, business counseling, basic banking services, and financial literacy training to underserved communities.

WHAT IS A CDFI?

The CDFI Fund serves communities primarily through the nationwide network of Community Development Financial Institutions, or CDFIs. CDFIs are <u>mission-driven</u> financial institutions <u>dedicated to community development</u> and provide financial services and products to meet the needs of <u>economically disadvantaged individuals within underserved communities</u>.

In order to become a certified CDFI, an organization must meet the following seven statutory and regulatory criteria:

1. Be a legal entity;

2. Have a primary mission of promoting community development;

3. Serve principally an investment area or targeted population;

4. Be an insured depository institution, or otherwise have the offering of financial products and services as its predominant business activity;

5. Provide development services (such as technical assistance or counseling) in conjunction with its financing activity;

6. Maintain accountability to its target market; and

7. Be a non-governmental entity and not be controlled by any governmental entities.

TYPES OF CDFIs

There are several different types of CDFIs, but all of them share the common mission of serving low-income communities.

Loan funds

Credit unions

Banks

Venture capital funds

CDFIs PROVIDE A VARIETY OF FINANCIAL SERVICES, INCLUDING:

- Loans and investments for small businesses, affordable housing projects, community facilities, and commercial real estate;

- Retail banking products and services for low- and moderate-income consumers; and

- Development services, such as business planning, credit counseling, and financial education, to help their borrowers use credit effectively.

CDFI RECERTIFICATION

In 2013, the CDFI Fund carried out a comprehensive recertification effort involving the majority of CDFIs. This effort ensured that organizations continue to meet the criteria required of all certified CDFIs, thereby enabling them to participate in the CDFI Fund's programs. Over the year, the CDFI Fund recertified 425 CDFIs and certified 76 new CDFIs. At the end of FY 2013, there were 811 Certified CDFIs, including 67 Native CDFIs:

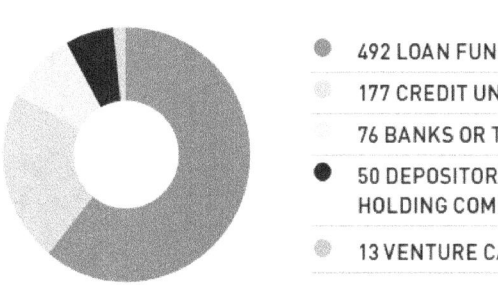

- 492 LOAN FUNDS
- 177 CREDIT UNIONS
- 76 BANKS OR THRIFTS
- 50 DEPOSITORY INSTITUTION HOLDING COMPANIES
- 13 VENTURE CAPITAL FUNDS

THE CDFI FUND'S BUDGET

The U.S. Congress appropriates the CDFI Fund's budget on an annual basis. The budget is divided between program and administrative expenses. Program funds are used for program awards – grants, loans, deposits, equity investments, and capacity building. Administrative funds are used to cover the costs to administer all CDFI Fund programs, including the NMTC Program and the CDFI Bond Guarantee Program. However, the tax credits themselves are authorized separately and the guarantees are provided at no net cost to the government.

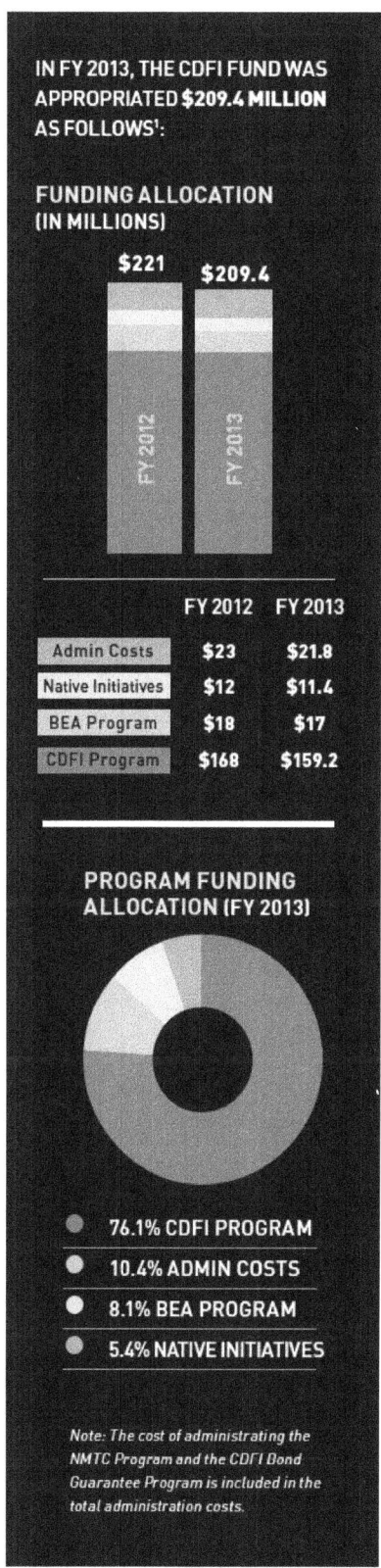

IN FY 2013, THE CDFI FUND WAS APPROPRIATED **$209.4 MILLION** AS FOLLOWS[1]:

FUNDING ALLOCATION (IN MILLIONS)

$221 — FY 2012
$209.4 — FY 2013

	FY 2012	FY 2013
Admin Costs	$23	$21.8
Native Initiatives	$12	$11.4
BEA Program	$18	$17
CDFI Program	$168	$159.2

PROGRAM FUNDING ALLOCATION (FY 2013)

- 76.1% CDFI PROGRAM
- 10.4% ADMIN COSTS
- 8.1% BEA PROGRAM
- 5.4% NATIVE INITIATIVES

Note: The cost of administering the NMTC Program and the CDFI Bond Guarantee Program is included in the total administration costs.

THANK YOU, DONNA GAMBRELL!

Thank you Donna Gambrell for your dedicated public service! 37 years of Federal service and six years as CDFI Fund Director.

ENTERED FEDERAL SERVICE – 10/6/1976
APPOINTED AS CDFI FUND DIRECTOR – 11/9/2007
RETIRED FROM FEDERAL SERVICE – 12/28/2013

In December 2013, the CDFI Fund said farewell to Donna Gambrell, its longest-serving director and the first African-American woman to lead the organization. Director Gambrell was head of the CDFI Fund for six years, steering its efforts to support CDFIs, CDEs, and underserved communities through one of the most difficult economic periods in recent history.

Director Gambrell capably focused the CDFI Fund's efforts to respond to the economic crisis, managing the CDFI Fund's participation in the American Recovery and Reinvestment Act of 2009 and overseeing the launch of new award programs and initiatives, such as the Capital Magnet Fund and the Healthy Food Financing Initiative, to better support low-income communities and the financial institutions that serve them. During her tenure, the CDFI Fund's appropriations quadrupled, paving the way for increased awards under the flagship CDFI Program and the beginning of the Capacity Building Initiative, the CDFI Fund's first focused training series for the CDFI industry.

One of Director Gambrell's final achievements before her retirement from federal service was standing up the CDFI Bond Guarantee Program, which greatly expanded the financing possibilities of CDFIs and has the potential to shape the direction of the CDFI industry for years to come. It is fitting that since Director Gambrell dedicated her tenure at the CDFI Fund to expanding its impact and focusing its directives, she would spend her last few months positioning the CDFI Fund for future success, leaving it stronger than ever.

FY 2013 AT A GLANCE

TOP FINANCIAL DATA

While statistics reflect the scale of the work that CDFIs and CDEs have accomplished over FY 2013 and since inception, the true stories lie within the communities impacted by these investments. Each investment made is a commitment by the CDFI Fund and the CDFI to build a better future.

FY 2013 DATA [2,3]

COMMUNITY INVESTMENT

$493.5 MILLION
The increase in amount spent on community development projects by BEA Program applicants over their prior year's investment in these types of projects, up from $432.4 million during the FY 2012 round.

$4.8 BILLION
The amount in loans and investments made possible through the NMTC Program, of which 79 percent were in severely distressed communities, up from 70 percent in CY 2011.

$325 MILLION
The amount in approved term sheets and agreements to guarantee executed through the CDFI Bond Guarantee Program in FY 2013.

BUSINESSES

6,558
The number of businesses financed by CDFI Program awardees, up from 4,102 in FY 2011.

491
The number of businesses financed by NMTC allocatees, down from 578 in CY 2011.

CERTIFIED CDFIs

76
The number of new CDFIs certified in FY 2013.

425
The number of CDFIs recertified in FY 2013.

811
Total number of certified CDFIs at the end of FY 2013, including 67 Native CDFIs.

[2]Source: CDFI Fund FY 2013 Annual Financial Report
[3]NMTC Program investments have leveled off since the additional $3 billion in allocation authority made possible through the American Recovery and Reinvestment Act.

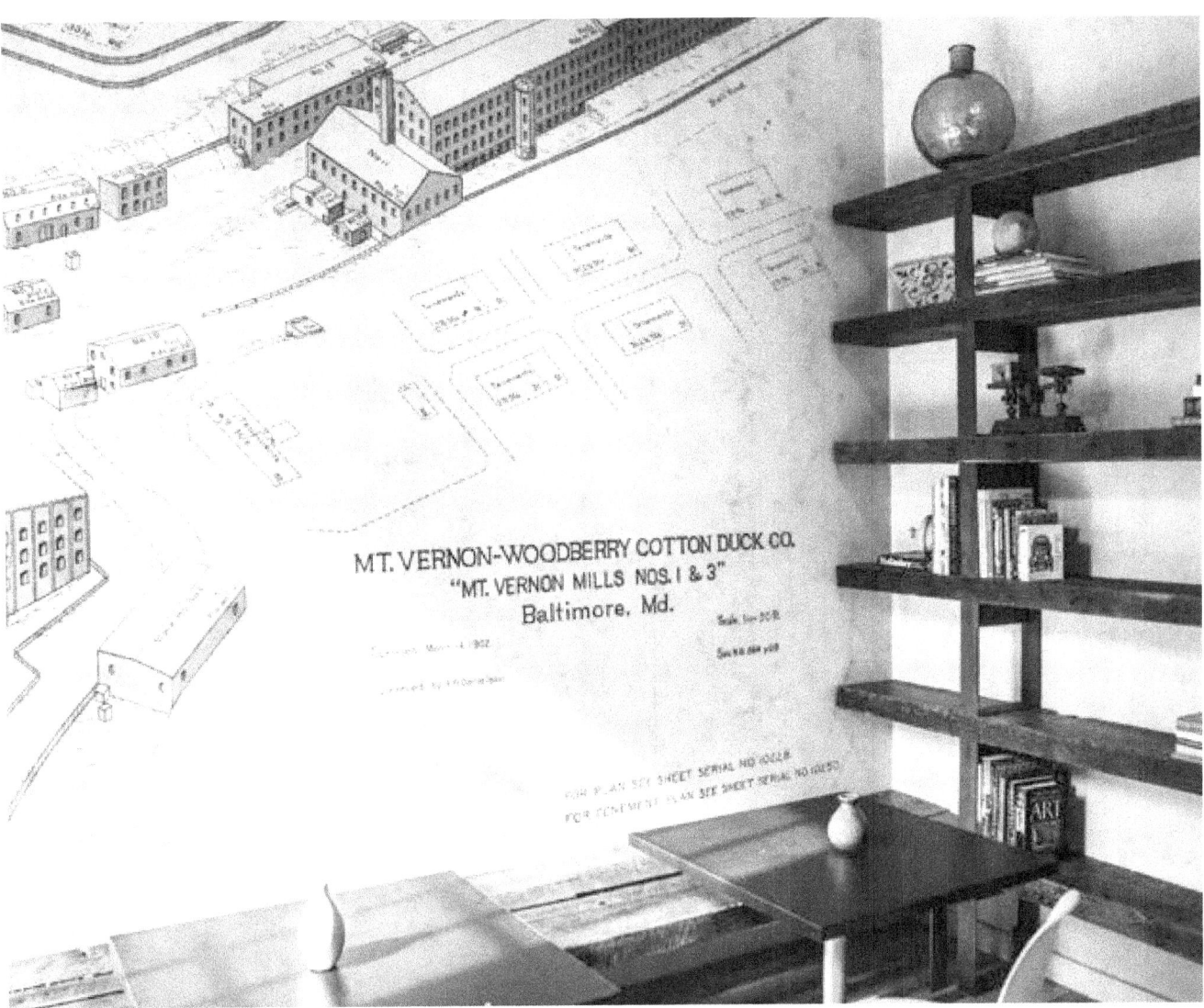

MT. VERNON-WOODBERRY COTTON DUCK CO.
"MT. VERNON MILLS NOS. I & 3"
Baltimore, Md.

HOUSING AND COMMERCIAL REAL ESTATE

$14.4 MILLION

The amount of square feet of commercial real estate developed from financing from NMTC allocatees, down from 18.6 million in CY 2011.

1,856

The number of affordable housing units financed by NMTC allocatees, down from 2,967 in CY 2011.

17,732

The number of affordable housing units financed by CDFI Program awardees, down from 24,466 in FY 2011.

JOBS

The number of jobs created or maintained through CDFI Program awardees, up from 25,618 in FY 2011.

The number of jobs created from the funds deployed through the NMTC Program down from 31,405 in CY 2011.

KEY HISTORICAL DATA[4]

CDFI PROGRAM, NACA PROGRAM AND BEA PROGRAM

$1.9 BILLION
The total amount that the CDFI Fund awarded since its creation in 1994.

$1.4 BILLION
The total amount of the CDFI Program and NACA Program awards.

$371 MILLION
The total amount of the BEA Program awards.

3,072
The total number of hours of technical assistance that have been provided to CDFIs since the Capacity Building Initiative was created in 2011.

NMTC PROGRAM

$36.5 BILLION
The total amount that the CDFI Fund awarded in tax credit allocation authority through the NMTC Program since its enactment in 2000.

4,706
The total number of businesses financed by NMTC Program allocatees, up from 1,781 in CY 2011.

11,730
The total number of affordable housing units developed from financing from NMTC Program allocatees, up from 7,488 in CY 2011.

$149.2 MILLION
The total amount of square feet of commercial real estate developed from financing from NMTC Program allocatees, up from 109.3 million in CY 2011.

207,550
The total number of jobs created from the equity raised and deployed through the NMTC Program, up from 111,277 in CY 2011.

⁴ Source: CDFI Fund FY 2013 Annual Financial Report

PROGRAM ACHIEVEMENTS

COMMUNITY DEVELOPMENT FINANCIAL INSTITUTIONS PROGRAM

www.cdfifund.gov/cdfi

The Community Development Financial Institutions Program (CDFI Program) is the primary federal grant program for CDFIs. The CDFI Program invests in and builds the capacity of CDFIs nationwide, empowering them to grow, achieve organizational sustainability, and contribute to the revitalization of the communities that they serve. CDFIs make specific investment decisions based on local needs and opportunities.

In FY 2013, the CDFI Program instituted a streamlined application process after extensive research and an in-depth look at feedback from previous public comments. The new application reduces the burden of data entry and is now more user-friendly. Additionally, webinars help CDFIs during the application process with step-by-step instructions for completing the application.

There are two types of monetary awards given through the CDFI Program: Financial Assistance and Technical Assistance. CDFIs use these funds to:

- Promote economic development by supporting small businesses, creating jobs, and developing commercial real estate.

- Develop affordable housing and promote home ownership.

- Provide financial services, including basic banking services, financial literacy programs and alternatives to predatory lending.

Since the program's inception in 1994, organizations have received over $1.4 billion in Financial Assistance and Technical Assistance.

THE CDFI PROGRAM AWARDED $172.6 MILLION TO CDFIS IN FY 2013.

FINANCIAL ASSISTANCE AWARDS

Financial Assistance awards are made in the form of investments, loans, deposits, and grants to help existing CDFIs.

Any CDFI that receives a Financial Assistance award through the Core component or the Healthy Food Financing Initiative must match the amount dollar-for-dollar with non-federal funds. This enables CDFIs to leverage outside resources to most effectively serve their economically distressed communities with increased lending.

IN FY 2013, THE CDFI FUND RECEIVED FINANCIAL ASSISTANCE **APPLICATIONS FROM 303 COMMUNITY ORGANIZATIONS** REQUESTING MORE THAN **$395.5 MILLION** IN FUNDING.

THROUGH A RIGOROUS SELECTION PROCESS, THE CDFI FUND AWARDED A TOTAL OF **$146.7 MILLION** TO **148 ORGANIZATIONS** THROUGHOUT THE U.S.

Since the demand for Financial Assistance is high, the CDFI Fund capped awards at $1.347 million in FY 2013 in an attempt to meet the heavy demand.

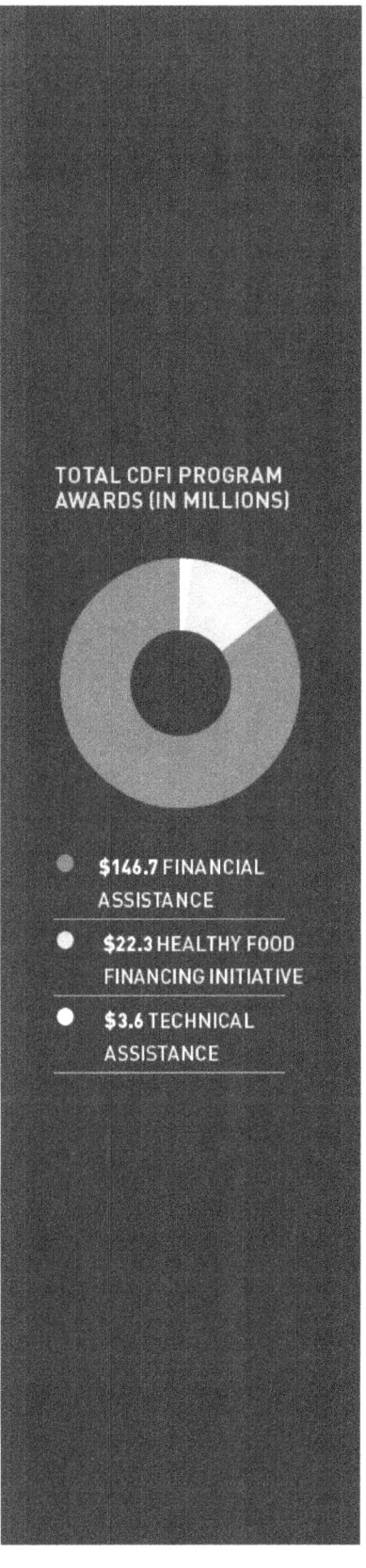

TOTAL CDFI PROGRAM AWARDS (IN MILLIONS)

- **$146.7** FINANCIAL ASSISTANCE
- **$22.3** HEALTHY FOOD FINANCING INITIATIVE
- **$3.6** TECHNICAL ASSISTANCE

HEALTHY FOOD FINANCING INITIATIVE

The Healthy Food Financing Initiative (HFFI) is a joint initiative between the U.S. Department of the Treasury, U.S. Department of Agriculture, and U.S. Department of Health and Human Services.

Through the HFFI, the CDFI Fund provides flexible technical and financial assistance awards to CDFIs that invest in businesses that provide healthy food options to help eliminate "food deserts."

In FY 2013, the CDFI Fund received applications from 35 eligible organizations requesting $84.8 million in HFFI Financial Assistance. The CDFI Fund awarded **$22.3 million in Financial Assistance Awards** in FY 2013 to help **10 CDFIs** finance healthy food activities.

TECHNICAL ASSISTANCE AWARDS

Technical Assistance awards are grants to build the capacity for both start-up and existing CDFIs. These grants are used for staff salaries, benefits, training, professional services, supplies, and equipment. Unlike the Financial Assistance awards, there are no matching requirements for these grants.

Newly certified CDFIs often use these funds to develop lending policies and procedures or to build staff lending capacity. More established CDFIs tend to use Technical Assistance awards to develop new products, serve their market in new ways or upgrade computer hardware or software.

THE CDFI FUND RECEIVED **86 TECHNICAL ASSISTANCE** APPLICATIONS IN FY 2013, REQUESTING MORE THAN **$8.1 MILLION** IN GRANTS.

AFTER THE CDFI FUND SELECTION PROCESS, **43 ORGANIZATIONS** WERE AWARDED A TOTAL OF **$3.6 MILLION**.

MEASURING SUCCESS

Financial Assistance and Technical Assistance awardees report their annual performance to the CDFI Fund. This helps local organizations and the CDFI Fund measure success and visualize impact.

ANNUAL PERFORMANCE OF CDFI PROGRAM AWARDEES[6]

Lending and Investing Activity	2012 Activity Reported in FY 2013
Total Loans/Investments Originated	$1.98 billion
Affordable Housing Units Financed	17,732 housing units
Businesses Financed	6,558 businesses
Percent of Eligible Areas Served	25.3%

The CDFI Fund commissioned the CDFI program evaluation in the summer of 2012 and the final report is due in 2014. Two university-based teams are conducting the research: The Carsey Institute of the University of New Hampshire, and Socratic Solutions, a firm affiliated with the Darden School of the University of Virginia. The evaluation examines a wide variety of methods and impact measures to determine the impact of the CDFI Program on its award recipients as well as the impact of award recipients on the communities they serve. This study should help identify how to improve and target the efforts by CDFIs to serve their target markets.

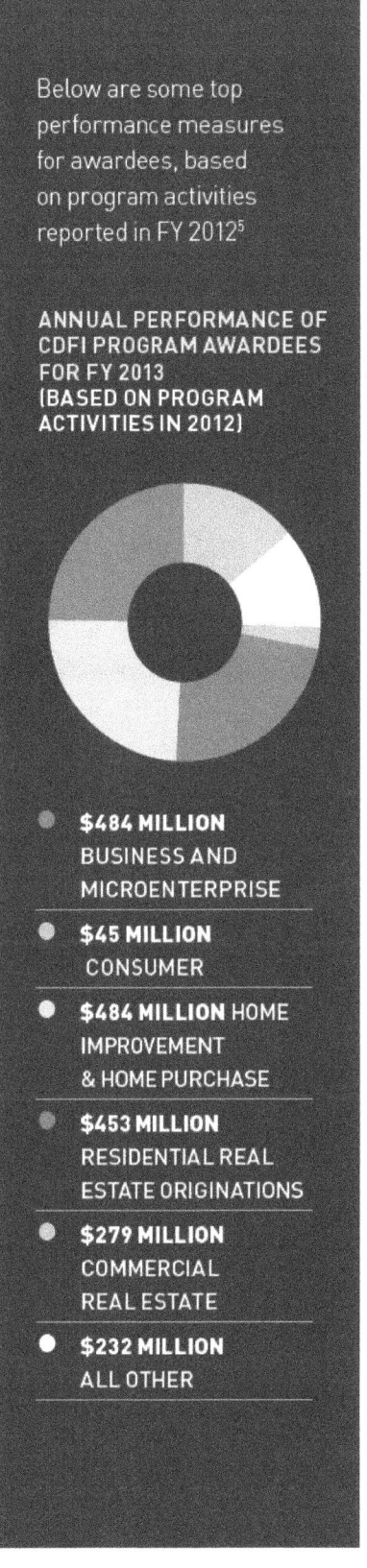

Below are some top performance measures for awardees, based on program activities reported in FY 2012[5]

ANNUAL PERFORMANCE OF CDFI PROGRAM AWARDEES FOR FY 2013 (BASED ON PROGRAM ACTIVITIES IN 2012)

$484 MILLION
BUSINESS AND MICROENTERPRISE

$45 MILLION
CONSUMER

$484 MILLION HOME IMPROVEMENT & HOME PURCHASE

$453 MILLION
RESIDENTIAL REAL ESTATE ORIGINATIONS

$279 MILLION
COMMERCIAL REAL ESTATE

$232 MILLION
ALL OTHER

[5]Source: CDFI Fund FY 2013 Annual Financial Report

[6]Source: CDFI Fund FY 2013 Annual Financial Report

CAPACITY BUILDING INITIATIVE

www.cdfifund.gov/cbi

The Capacity Building Initiative helps CDFIs improve their ability to deliver financial products and services to economically distressed communities and achieve long-term sustainability.

Through free training workshops, webinars, market research, customized technical assistance, and informational resources, the Capacity Building Initiative helps CDFIs develop, diversify, and grow.

The specialized trainings target important issues that affect CDFIs and the communities they serve, including affordable housing and business lending, portfolio management, risk assessment, foreclosure prevention, general business operations, liquidity and capitalization challenges, and more.

Training and technical assistance is provided on-site, in the communities where CDFIs work. Additional online resources and webinars are provided.

At the end of FY 2013, the CDFI Fund was administering six active training series and was in the midst of developing additional training options.

CAPACITY BUILDING INITIATIVE RESOURCE BANK

The Capacity Building Initiative Resource Bank is a virtual library of training curricula, webinars, subject-specific reference materials, and third-party research reports. Accessed through the CDFI Fund's website, the Resource Bank is a valuable resource that provides CDFIs and the general public with a one-stop source of information on subjects relevant to the current needs of the CDFI industry.

FY 2013 TRAINING SERIES (ACTIVE)

● ● ●

LEADERSHIP JOURNEY: NATIVE CDFI GROWTH AND EXCELLENCE

Supports the growth and long-term sustainability of Native CDFIs by helping leaders address the critical challenges of their specific organizations.

This training series will conclude in July 2015.

● ● ●

PRESERVING AND EXPANDING CDFI MINORITY DEPOSITORY INSTITUTIONS

Addresses the unique challenges facing CDFI Minority Depository Institutions by providing them advanced training and technical assistance.

This training series will conclude in December 2014.

● ● ●

FINANCING COMMUNITY HEALTH CENTERS

Provides advanced training, technical assistance, and forums for peer learning for CDFIs to establish and improve services for community health centers.

This training series will conclude in February 2015.

● ● ●

STRENGTHENING SMALL AND EMERGING CDFIS

Expands the capacity of small and emerging CDFIs through a comprehensive training and technical assistance program.

This training series will conclude in July 2014.

● ● ●

INNOVATIONS IN SMALL BUSINESS LENDING

Supports business-oriented CDFIs that are experienced in providing loans and services to small and medium-sized enterprises.

This training series concluded at the end of FY 2013.

● ● ●

SCALING UP MICROFINANCE

Helps expand the capacity of CDFIs that specialize in microfinance.

This training series will conclude at the end of calendar year 2014.

Over FY 2013, four of the training series held training events, webinars and provided technical assistance. They were the Leadership Journey, Strengthening Small and Emerging CDFIs, Innovations in Small Business Lending, and Scaling up Microfinance. These four produced the following outputs:

- 293 individuals who attended training events;

- 713 individuals who participated in webinars;

- 108 CDFIs that received direct Technical Assistance.

The first training events for the Community Health Centers and CDFI Minority Depository Institutions training series were held in the first quarter of FY 2014.

The CDFI Fund would like to thank the Opportunity Finance Network, NeighborWorks® America, and Deloitte Financial Advisory Services LLP for conducting the training sessions.

NATIVE INITIATIVES

www.cdfifund.gov/native

The Native Initiatives generates economic opportunity for Native Communities by supporting the creation and expansion of Native CDFIs, which in turn help to create jobs, establish or improve affordable housing, and provide appropriate financial services and counseling within their communities.

Native Communities, including Native American, Alaskan Native, and Native Hawaiian communities, face some of the greatest barriers to accessing capital and basic financial services in the nation. Specialized, mission-driven organizations (Native CDFIs) help these communities to grow by increasing their access to credit, capital, and financial services.

The Native Initiatives' central component is the Native American CDFI Assistance Program (NACA Program), which increases the number and capacity of existing or new CDFIs serving Native Communities.

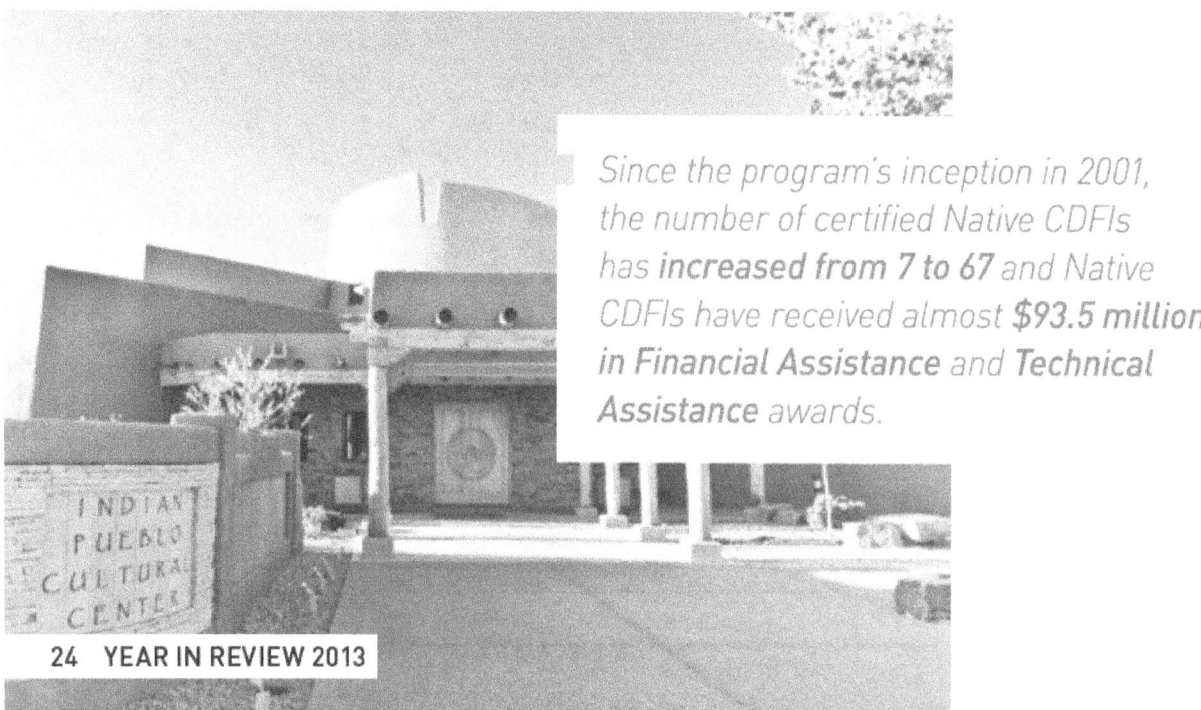

*Since the program's inception in 2001, the number of certified Native CDFIs has **increased from 7 to 67** and Native CDFIs have received almost **$93.5 million** in **Financial Assistance** and **Technical Assistance** awards.*

The performance results reported by NACA Program awardees in FY 2013 show Native CDFIs originated 1,508 loans or investments totaling $23.2 million based on their portfolio activities of 2012.

Native CDFIs focus largely on affordable housing and economic development.

IN FY 2013, THE CDFI FUND RECEIVED **59 NACA ELIGIBLE APPLICATIONS** REQUESTING A TOTAL OF **$24.3 MILLION** FOR BOTH FINANCIAL ASSISTANCE AND TECHNICAL ASSISTANCE FUNDING. THE CDFI FUND WAS ABLE TO PROVIDE AWARDS TO OVER HALF OF THE ELIGIBLE APPLICATIONS BY AWARDING **35 ORGANIZATIONS** A TOTAL OF **$12.4 MILLION** FOR BOTH FINANCIAL ASSISTANCE AND TECHNICAL ASSISTANCE FUNDING.

A NEW STUDY: "ACCESS TO CAPITAL & CREDIT IN NATIVE COMMUNITIES"

In 2013, the CDFI Fund announced the launch of a new study, "Access to Capital and Credit in Native Communities," which will identify the unique challenges that affect the availability of capital and credit for individuals and businesses in Native Communities to help overcome barriers to financial services.

The study will use a combination of existing research, Tribal consultations, and focus groups to identify important economic issues in Native Communities. To lead components of the study, the CDFI Fund has contracted with GBS, Inc., a wholly-owned subsidiary of Sitnasuak Native Corporation, a SBA-certified Alaskan Native 8(a) business.

NEW MARKETS TAX CREDIT PROGRAM

www.cdfifund.gov/nmtc

The New Markets Tax Credit Program (NMTC Program) helps economically distressed communities attract private investment capital. This federal tax credit helps to fill project financing gaps by enabling investors to make larger investments than would otherwise be possible. NMTC investments finance businesses and real estate projects in low-income communities.

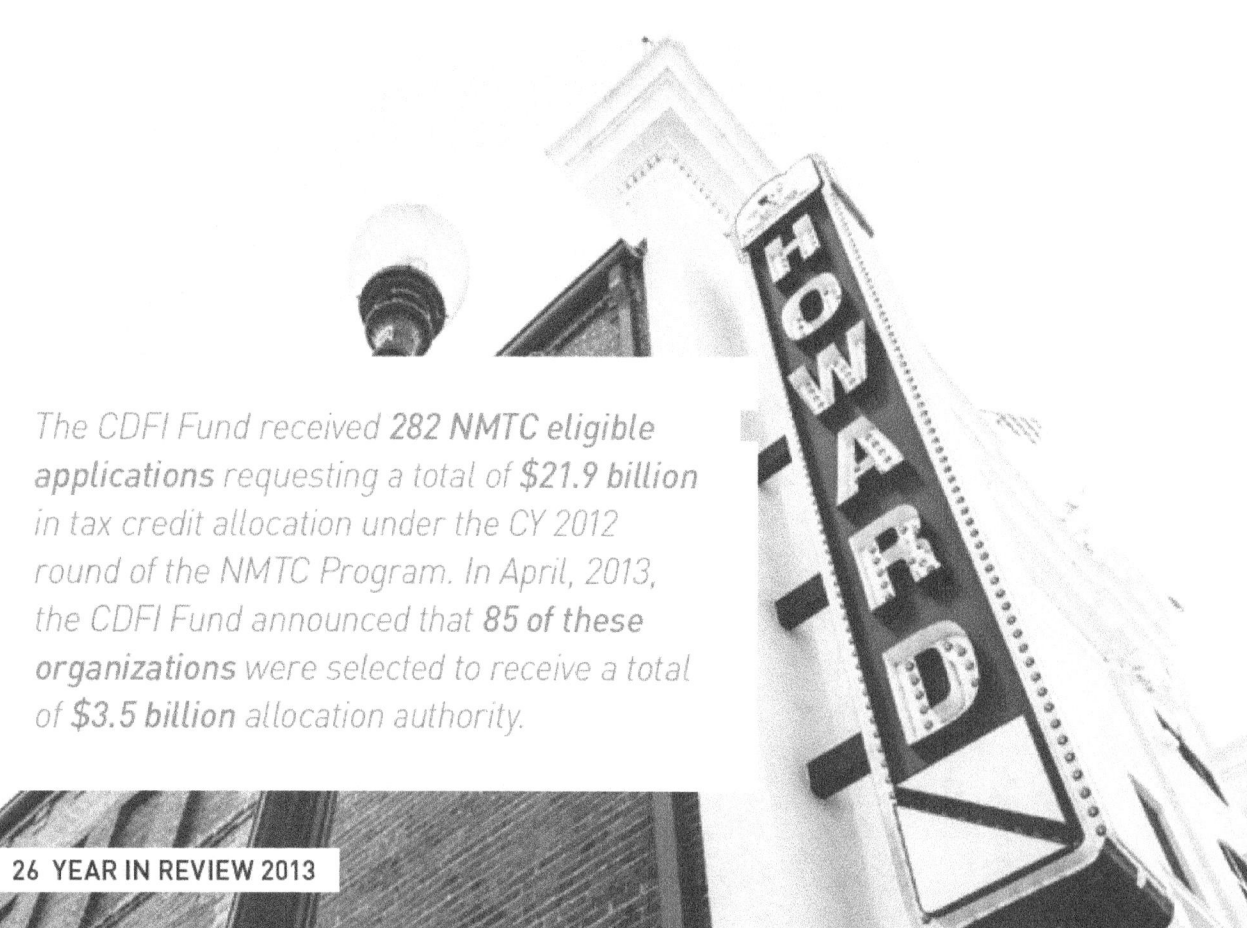

*The CDFI Fund received **282 NMTC eligible applications** requesting a total of **$21.9 billion** in tax credit allocation under the CY 2012 round of the NMTC Program. In April, 2013, the CDFI Fund announced that **85 of these organizations** were selected to receive a total of **$3.5 billion** allocation authority.*

The program permits taxpayers to receive a credit against federal income taxes for making Qualified Equity Investments (QEIs) in designated Community Development Entities (CDEs). The CDEs in turn use the capital raised to make investments in low-income communities, known as Qualified Low-Income Community Investments (QLICIs). The CDFI Fund is responsible for awarding tax credit allocation authority to CDEs.

Unlike the CDFI Fund's other programs, the NMTC Program operates on a calendar year schedule, not fiscal year, to parallel the tax year. Since the first allocation round in 2002:

- Demand for NMTC allocation authority has been very high, with 2,670 applications requesting tax credit authority for more than $251.2 billion in equity investments.

- The CDFI Fund has completed ten allocation rounds and has made 749 awards totaling $36.5 billion in tax credit allocation authority.

- This $36.5 billion includes $3 billion in Recovery Act Awards and $1 billion of special allocation authority to be used for the recovery and redevelopment of the Gulf Opportunity Zone.

In October 2013, the CDFI Fund announced it had received a total of 310 applications under the CY 2013 round of the NMTC Program requesting a total of $25.8 billion in NMTC allocation authority.

ANNUAL PERFORMANCE OF NMTC PROGRAM ALLOCATEES[7]

Note: Allocatees report QEI and loan/investment activity to the CDFI Funds through the Allocation Tracking System (ATS) and Community Investment Impact System (CIIS), respectively. Annual performance data represents the allocatees' CIIS data reported for FY 2013 (program year 2012).

[7]Source: CDFI Fund FY 2013 Annual Financial Report

[8]Qualified Low-Income Community Investments

BANK ENTERPRISE AWARD PROGRAM

www.cdfifund.gov/bea

The Bank Enterprise Award Program (BEA Program) awards FDIC-insured depository institutions for making investments in certified CDFIs and in the most distressed communities throughout the nation.

Approximately $371.4 million has been awarded through the BEA Program since its inception in 1994.

BEA Program awardees are recognized for increasing their investment in CDFIs and for increasing their loans and investments in communities where at least **30 percent of the population lives at or below the national poverty level** and where **unemployment is at least 1.5 times the national average**. Organizations that receive awards must then reinvest that money back into distressed communities.

FY 2013 BEA
PROGRAM AWARDS

In FY 2013, the BEA Program received 98 eligible applications requesting more than $91 million, compared to 71 applications requesting a total of $88.5 million in FY 2012.

In FY 2013, the CDFI Fund provided $17 million in BEA Program awards to 85 FDIC-insured depository institutions headquartered in 23 states and the District of Columbia. The average award was $200,574.

FY 2013 BEA COMMUNITY IMPACT

FY 2013 BEA Program applicants increased their qualified community development activities by $493.5 million over their prior year level of activities, including:

$493.5 MILLION

● **$427.8 MILLION**
INCREASE IN LOANS AND INVESTMENTS IN DISTRESSED COMMUNITIES

● **$55.4 MILLION**
INCREASE IN LOANS, DEPOSITS, AND TECHNICAL ASSISTANCE TO CDFIS; AND

● **$10.3 MILLION**
INCREASE IN THE PROVISION OF FINANCIAL SERVICES IN DISTRESSED COMMUNITIES.

CDFI BOND GUARANTEE PROGRAM

www.cdfifund.gov/bond

The CDFI Bond Guarantee Program was created through the Small Business Jobs Act of 2010, and will provide CDFIs access to a significant source of capital. By providing guarantees of bonds issued by certain qualified issuers, the CDFI Bond Guarantee Program will provide long-term capital for community development investments through a program that is designed to function at no cost to taxpayers.

This new program is transformational because CDFIs can gain from the potential scale of the CDFI Bond Guarantee Program, which offers long-term credit at attractive interest rates.

Through the CDFI Bond Guarantee Program, qualified entities (CDFIs or their designees) will issue bonds that are guaranteed by the federal government and use the bond proceeds to extend or refinance credit to CDFIs. The CDFIs use these funds to make loans in underserved communities.

The Secretary of the Treasury may guarantee up to 10 bonds per year, each at a minimum of $100 million, and the total of all bonds cannot exceed $1 billion per year.

Unlike other CDFI Fund programs, the CDFI Bond Guarantee Program is a "self-pay" initiative. Participating CDFIs take on a debt obligation that must be repaid. The program's pooled lending structure allows for greater flexibility and participation among CDFIs while balancing overall lending risk for the Federal Financing Bank, the bond purchaser.

The U.S. Department of the Treasury announced in September 2013 that it has approved term sheets and executed agreements to guarantee for **$325 million in bonds** with maturities up to 29.5 years. The FY 2013 round was the inaugural round of the CDFI Bond Guarantee Program.

The **four Eligible CDFIs** that were approved to participate in the inaugural round of the CDFI Bond Guarantee Program are:

- Clearinghouse CDFI

- Enterprise Community Loan Fund, Inc.

- Local Initiatives Support Corporation

- The Community Development Trust, LP

The **three organizations** that have been selected to serve as the **Qualified Issuers** are:

- Opportunity Finance Network

- The Community Reinvestment Fund

- TriSail Funding Corporation (a Bank of America affiliate).

FY 2014
STRATEGIC PRIORITIES

As we reflect upon the remarkable achievements of the CDFI Fund in FY 2013, we still have an eye to the future and continue to constantly strive to better the organization and create new strategic goals for the future.

BOND GUARANTEE APPROVAL

Providing up to $750 million in guarantees for bonds issued under the CDFI Bond Guarantee Program.

CDFI CERTIFICATION

Continuing efforts to ensure that CDFIs maintain their certification status and implement annual reporting for all certified CDFIs. These actions will ensure the integrity of CDFI certification as a brand.

COMPLIANCE

Continuing compliance risk research and program evaluation of the effectiveness of CDFI Fund programs.

RELATIONSHIPS

Fostering intergovernmental, non-profit, and private-sector partnerships to further leverage resources for CDFIs.

OPERATIONS

Developing and reevaluating policies and processes to streamline operations and improve administrative efficiency and efficacy.

PHOTO CREDITS

CDFI FUND

1801 L STREET NW
6TH FLOOR
WASHINGTON, DC 20220

CDFIFUND.GOV

www.ingramcontent.com/pod-product-compliance
Lightning Source LLC
Chambersburg PA
CBHW080733290526
45790CB00008B/3169